GRAFFITI REVISITED

By

Benedict Nnolim

Published September 2013

ISBN 978-1-906914-97-4

Ben Nnolim Books
7 Sandway Path,
St. Mary Cray, Orpington.
Kent BR5 3TS, UK
bnbs@ymail.com

Benedict Nnolim: GRAFFITI REVISITED

Table of Contents

Benedict Nnolim: GRAFFITI REVISITED

DEDICATION

This book is dedicated to all those who wish the
world well and to genuine Christians, who have
become an endangered species in the modern world.

PREFACE

The precursor edition, of GRAFFITI REVISITED, GRAFFITI, was a shocked reaction to the sobering realization that, in spite of the phenomenal progress the human race seems to have made, nothing seems to have changed in the conduct of both private and public human affairs, confirming the Biblical saying, attributed to King Solomon, that there is nothing new under the sun (Ecclesiastes 1: 9; RSV).

Perhaps, this is the consequence of tick box education, which became mainstream from the 1960s, in which sustained, reasoned, thinking was discarded for quick, sometimes, guess work, multiple choice, answers. Maybe, it is the consequence of the natural law of decay, deterioration and decadence, articulated, scientifically, by the so called second law of thermodynamics which states that all natural processes are irreversible, that no natural process can be 100 % efficient, or that the entropy of the universe always increases in a natural process, affirming what God was reported to have said to Adam and Eve in Paradise "……*you are dust and to dust you shall return*" (Genesis Chapter 3 verse 19, RSV).

All the current hullabaloo and the associated populist legislation in favour of human rights, abortion, same sex marriage and society approved and encouraged hedonism and materialism are merely echoes, and incidences in our time, of cyclical reoccurrences of previous and ancient debates, conflicts or battles that were won against, and lost to, societal realization of the need for order, discipline and coherence in social behavior and interaction.

What is constant, and never seems to change, is that there is always a small minority of persons and groups who lament, struggle to prevent, to reverse or postpone, what appears to be too hasty a stampede of humanity, against all received sense and reason, to self-destruction.

GRAFFITI REVISITED is one of such struggles, and is a review, and rewriting of some, of the poems in the earlier edition, together with the introduction of new poems written before and since the first GRAFFITI edition.

Benedict Nnolim
September 7, 2013

Chapter One

PLEASANT MALE AND FEMALE KINDS

It may be bad, it may be good,
it all depends on your point of view.
But what I know, of this I'm sure,
it hasn't done us very much good.

To be nice and pleasant male,
is praised, extolled, by all.
What a lady, nice to know,
music, sweet, to the female ear.

There's no party that is held
without their being the hub of it.
Tales of triumph, joy or woe,
attack, bombard, their patient ears.

But what a toll that all these take
on pleasant male and female kind,
with no time or space for self,
no time to rest in private space.

It's now I see, it dawns on me,
why my friends are not so nice.
To self-preserve - a law of life -
better sane than a popular wreck.

TELLING THE TRUTH

Has there ever been a time
when telling the truth was not,

at best,
an occupational hazard,
but most times,
a dangerous enterprise
that takes its toll on,
and, even, costs, lives?

From ancient times, middle times,
to modern times,
those, who dared to tell the truth,
have had themselves, their kith and kin,
to blame.

Talking of truth,
what, indeed, is truth?
So many things, so many needs,
and so many wants,
need, want and yearn to be the truth.

That lies, deceit and all kinds of falsehoods,
camouflage and pose as truth;
and, often, more than truth itself,
convince the throng, in righteous rage,
to inflict their dastardly acts on truth.

That, outflanked, oppressed and tarred,
truth, itself, is dressed in shame;
shouted down, not even heard,
its tiny voice, in opprobrium, drowned,
its bloodied and battered body,
buried in tons of filthy mud.

Yet, this truth, it never dies,

even if its bearers do.
Yes, this truth, it never dies,
even as generations come and go.

In its time, it rears its head,
in shining splendour,
enrobed in wondrous light,
it shines so bright
that all are forced to see,
and watch and marvel at the sight.

Tongues are tied, mouths agape;
guilt, regret, and shame is felt by all,
who ostracized and killed their kind,
because of, and on behalf of,
strident and cunning lies,
disguised as truth.

None dares to point at,
or admit, their shame,
to the public they deceived.
Even those, who died for truth, don't rejoice;
vindication gives no joy.

Truth took too much time,
it took too long,
to make its triumph clear to all.
While it dallied,
we died and lost our lives,
in pain and tears, telling the truth.

If those who lied, and cursed,
oppressed and tarred the truth,

now eat humble pies,
we're not amused,
because, now, we know
and see and feel,
what King Pyrrhus must have known,
seen and felt.

DIALOGUE

Dialogue! Dialogue!
Oh! The Greeks and their *logos*!
Socrates, he talked of it;
did he not end up with it?

Julius Caesar, he was smart;
he had no time for such an art.
No Greek thoughts, at least, not when
Roma will *locuta est*.

But the British and the French,
when they heard of it, at first,
with their kith and kin and kind,
looked and looked but satirised.

When, at last, they found it out,
in all its kinds and in their tongues,
they made sure, first, their might was right
before they sailed to show the light.

They spread the news to all the lands;
to China, Asia, Africa.
Australasia, Pacific ;
everywhere was pacified.

When the Indians heard of it,
they turned around and changed their kith
to USA and Canada,
to get the best of dialogue.

Africans were short of it;
fighting, killing, eating, each
of their kind because, in truth,
they did not know it, not a bit.

Now they're grown in dialogue.
See? Their lives are now a song.
Swimming in their dialogue,
happy as they die along.

Few examples will suffice
to tell the tale, it is profound.
When they take your wife by force,
you must come and dialogue.

When from home you're forced to run,
you must wait and dialogue.
See Iraq, Afghanistan,
each of them has dialogued.

So, my friends, I, here, propound
that all our life is dialogue.
And if your might is not so sound,
be prepared to dialogue.

GOOD AND EVIL

Good is good;

evil is bad;
in between
there are many things.

There is black;
there is white;
in between
a lot of grey.

Name a thing,
anything,
good or bad
or in between.

And let me know
of even one,
whose seeds, in youth,
we did not sow.

All the problems of this life,
sown as seeds in tender youth,
in later life to blossom new,
from the choices made by us.

The road to Hell, the pundits say,
is paved with good intentions here.
A saying sounding wise and true,
its falsehood masked by brazenness.

A falsehood, novel, glib, profane,
a populist joke on sacredness,
muddling truth and common sense,
the point, our minds, by these, confuse.

The truth must be, or so they say,
that the tunes, the best of them,
are the devils' copyrights-
Satan's, Lucifer's, Beelzebub's.

The biggest saint cannot resist
a stifled chuckle at his jests,
leading next to great remorse,
paid in penance for the sin.

Choices made or forced on us,
these, the bane of human kind.
Eve, we're told, was faced with one,
so was Adam in his prime.

Human thought has, since, begot
so many thoughts and views on choice.
Starting right from ancients' thoughts
we've reached the choice we call informed.

To be informed, my, that is rare,
and rarer still in tender age,
not to mention time and place
and the welfare of your house.

Ignorance is much maligned
and blamed for choices of its kind.
Ill will and its evil kinds,
who will admit his evil mind?

Ignorance, in olden days,
a way of life for many folk,
lacking contact, out of touch,

their daily needs their guides to choice.

Now, it's hard to, still, believe
that choices made are ill informed.
What with iPads, TV sets,
and all the Press and News combined.

It is time we looked askance
at our lives and modern thought.
It is time we faced the truth
of good and evil and our choice.

I know I'm bound to get the flak
from modern logic and its facts;
for such a view is, well, unheard,
in terms of norms of modern thought.

I will not go back in time
to us remind of human kind,
who have had their modern thoughts,
but, now, in time and sands, are lost.

All the point I want to make
is as simple as its words.
Evil is bad, good is good;
all our choices are from them.

MORTAL SINS AND VENIAL SINS

Mortal sins and venial sins;
have you thought of what they do;
how they taunt and try our lives,
telling what our end will be?

Most of it is caused by Faith
and our yearnings to be safe.
There is fear, nay awe, that's aught
in a life that gives us fright.

Christians, Jews, they have their own,
so do Muslims, Hindus too.
They give them names, all different
names,
just to show it's not the same.

Ask the Buddhists what they think;
their Noble Truths and Eightfold Paths
will make you think of Beatitudes;
Heaven, though, they will not ask.

Ten Commandments of the Jews
are, for Christians, valid too,
who will add their Beatitudes,
loving friend and foe for Christ.

Muslims have their Pillars, five;
their lives, Jihads, a daily task.
Serving Allah with your might
is a must for Paradise.

Brahman is, for Hindus, all,
Taking all and various forms –
Vishnu, Shiva, Shakti, gods,
Karma, Yoga, Castes and all.

The list is long and that's the point
in many Faiths and their beliefs.

Those list will bore, I must admit;
without ado I make my point.

My point is simple, not profound –
when you're young and faced with
choice,
you want to know and know for sure
which is mortal, which venial.

If you're lucky and can tell
which is which of many sins;
you may run from mortal sins
and end your life in venial sins.

If confused by love and Faith
and cannot tell which one is which;
you will run from venial sins
and end your life in mortal sins.

If, from start, you do not care,
matching sins to your desire,
putting Faith behind your wants,
your end will be a throw of dice.

MANY THINGS WE THINK ARE MYTHS

Many things we think are myths;
when you come to think of it,
and go beyond the face of it,
make you wonder – are they myths?

I dare not bore you with the list
in many lands and many Faiths.

So many cultures, every age,
one and all, they have their myths.

There's one myth that, just, won't die;
Christians, Jews, for it, would die.
Their lives and fates are built on it;
it changed the world for good or ill.

It is there in Chapter One,
maybe Two or even Three,
in the book of Genesis,
in the Bible of the Jews.

In every age there is debate
and doubt and faith in what it says;
there's agreement, there's dissent,
truth and myth in constant test.

It talks of Adam and of Eve;
both were put in Paradise.
Fax this fast to modern times;
does it sound, still, like a myth?

Is it not the truth of life,
felt with pain, at times, with joy,
our womenfolk, their enterprise,
always fast and a step ahead?

Be they lady, wench or wife,
drenched in wealth and love and gifts,
true to type, like mother Eve,
are they ever satisfied?

11

Take the deeds of men since then;
though it's clear in Genesis,
male and female He made them,
in His image, only one.

But the men they thought it wise
to make the women of their choice,
to lord and master as they liked,
not as ones in God's design.

See the trouble that is caused.
Count the woes the world has seen.
See the groping in the dark
ignoring truth in search of myth.

POSH ELITE

Oh! The world I knew is gone.
Now, it's just a merry ball,
hurtling, rolling round in space,
giving sense no breathing space.

Today, it is a mortal sin
to be posh or some elite;
and this in spite of what we know,
it was elites that let us know.

Unpolished talk and commonness,
who, on earth, have these advanced?
Shameful envies of the past
have gained respect in public angst.

Genteel counsel and demand

are, now, derided by the throng.
Assertiveness and violent hands
will get you what you want from all.

Newly rich, irreverent,
assured that nature has been had,
wonder why they're still as guests.
Posh elite let's have you back.

NICE PEOPLE

People are not nice.
Don't get me wrong; there are nice people;
there are, even, people who are very nice.
But these are few and far between.

Being nice is just a game,
which, it seems, you have to play,
if you want to get along;
easier too than being, really, nice.

All you have to do,
is to look, or appear to be, nice,
talk and act as if you're nice,
none of which is hard to do.

Even if you tell a lie,
tell it nicely and with charm.
Even if you ruin a name,
do it nicely and with style.

Woe betide you, in your days,
if you do not play the game,

13

or lose concentration in your game.
I dare not tell you of your fate.

If you ever tell a truth, any truth,
you will find, indeed, in truth,
how wicked, nasty, intolerant,
these nice and gentle people, really, are.

PREJUDICE

A bully's illness at its worst,
a family sickness where they're born.
So bad and shameful it's unheard,
it had to hide in camouflage.

If this camouflage will work,
a good scapegoat, a likely word,
must be found to take the rap;
what better word than prejudice?

Prejudice is prejudgement;
through our lives, it's what we do.
We think, we talk, we implement,
not before we judge its good.

What we see and what we do
must, from start, be pigeonholed.
If it isn't classified,
we won't believe it makes a sense.

At times we're right,
at times we're wrong;
without prejudging,

we are lost.

My view, of it, you may dispute;
any step you take in life
must be done with prejudice,
if you do not want to die.

Prejudice, in life, is it.
We do not jump before we see.
If the facts, at last, don't fit,
in bad results, it's prejudice.

In all our lives, it does its part
in great discoveries and the arts.
It makes our thinking coherent
and helps decipher nature's kinds.

There is nothing wrong with thoughts
or prejudgement of our choice.
Life is nought without our thoughts
and, quite, unsafe without forethought

It helps us too, in strange surrounds,
to feel secure amid unknowns.
Whites and Blacks and all the sins;
terrible illness blamed on it.

You hurt, you hang, discriminate,
those you think are not like you,
or are weak, unversed in sin,
in jest, for business or for trade.

You won't admit you're sick and ill.

You find a name for your evil deeds.
You call your illness, prejudice,
and seek a cure by fighting it.

It is unfair to prejudice
to blame these terrible sins on it.
It is a sickness at its peak,
camouflaged as prejudice.

Kid yourself as you would like,
but leave prejudgement out of it.
For what you are you won't admit;
you are sick not prejudiced.

BIGOTS

Tentacles in search for peace,
ever, ever at their reach,
are numbed and burnt in times like these.

All the smarting we suppress,
all the wrath and passion boiled,
all are stirred and stoked by them.

They know not, really, what they do;
their hearts and minds in twisted knots;
these men and women of a past.

If we did not know them well,
their soul's frustration in a veil,
helpless victims in a tide.

If we placed their ways of thought

on the planes on which they're found,
the human race will be in shame.

Had we not been trained before,
by much experience that is past,
to smart and sigh in place of war,
can they live the way they are?

If we did not know before
to rule the ego, fancy prone,
with a reason tried and true,
what of peace and brotherhood?

All the things we ever learnt;
all the virtues and their aims;
all the pains we bore to learn
will just be efforts made in vain.

Because we, all, will join and fight,
the bloody war to maim and die;
in futile hope to teach the sense
that love and peace are best.

THE GODLY KIND

Of all the kinds, in modern times,
the most oppressed, the Godly kind.
It doesn't matter who their God
their main offence - they have a God.

To have a God is to bind yourself
to rules and life you may not like.
This is bad in modern times

where the rule is selfishness.

The Godly kind are not much fun;
their lives are full of dos and don'ts.
This is sin and this is wrong;
how, on earth, can life be fun?

What is life if not of fun?
What is life without a pun?
How can one go through this life,
always careful and in strife?

But these, contend the Godly kind,
are the reasons for their life.
Life is good and lots of fun,
if all of us are part of God.

Think of it, a world of love,
and all desires are of God.
There's no greed; there's no lust.
In all you do you want to be just.

There's no fear of being betrayed.
There's no fear of cheats.
No one tells a lie or fibs.
Every deal is fair and square.

To add to these, and when you die,
you will go to Paradise,
whose greatest treat must, surely, be
face to face and there with God.

But the rest, the ungodly kind,

think that all of this is bunk.
That is why, in modern times,
life is hard for the Godly kind.

THE CATHOLIC CHURCH

There are citizens everywhere
in every country of the world.
Some are thieves, some are rogues,
most are decent, lawful folks.

Every country has its laws
culture, mores and more.
The good, the lawful, in high regard;
the crooks are punished when they're caught.

Every country has its clubs,
and groups and places of their kinds.
Every club and place has its rules
for its members to behave.

Football clubs, cricket clubs,
all tennis and boxing clubs;
nobody tells them who will play
or the rules with which they play

In every club, its rules enforced,
in internal processes.
PhDs, and most degrees
are not given by the Press.

All of these I must admit
are for the world and life on earth.

There is no talk of afterlife
except for your kith and kin.

Pity then the Catholic Church,
whose membership is a group of three,
with one group down here on earth,
the other two in afterlife.

The good, industrious, get rewards,
not in life but when they die.
The lawless, punished, out of sight,
not in life but when they die.

With these constraints, it's quite a job
to get its members, here, to behave.
Its faith is all in Jesus Christ
by whom assured it won't be lost.

Its rules are hard but not beyond
its serious members reach.
But those its rules who often breach
would run as hares and chase as hounds.

To be a Catholic is their aim
while the rules they will not keep.
They want to change the Catholic Church
to suit their aims, within their reach.

Their kinds are found in every place,
much like germs in cleaned up space.
They ruin, infest, and bring to rot,
everything they come to touch.

Once they bring the Church to rot,
you would think they're good and done.
No. They move to another club,
to ruin, infest, and bring to rot.

Take a guess at who they use
to publicise misguided views.
It is the Press both free and fair
to sell the papers, adverts, fare.

The Press would like the Catholic Church
to sing and dance its tune;
to install the priests and Popes it likes
and make its rules of right and wrong.

What is Church, if not a crowd,
that has to live and move with times?
What is God if not a myth,
that cannot block the profit lines?

LAYERS OF TRUTH

Layers of truth, like onion skins,
are pealed, revealed, by life's travails.
Yet, unlike those tender skins,
their days and numbers never end.

Each new day and each new year,
a truth profound reveals itself.
And that is why it must be true
in God we'll find the final truth.

HIDDEN WARS

We hear the Greeks and Sisyphus,
the Romans, too, Tantalus.
We hear the Christians, Muslims too,
who talk of Satan, Lucifer.

I am sure there's more to hear,
in ancient, middle, modern times.
I cannot say they know themselves,
or may, in fact, be foes.

But what I see, it seems so clear,
there may be wars, unknown to us.

Chapter Two

GOD CONSTRUCTS

There are some you can't convince
that the world, and we in it,
are made by God and God alone.
All its wonders big and small,
stars, galaxies, suns and moons,
things unknown or yet to be known,
for all they care, are chance events.

Some of us are not well read;
for us this life is hard enough.
Oppressed by wants and needs and cares,
we can't afford, nor have the time
for foolish, idle, and vain thoughts,
especially, against our only hope -
the only thing that keeps us on -
God.

Some of us are very well read,
convinced, and sure, we know it all.
Our comfortable lives are proof, in fact,
that all our views are right.
So we say, with certainty,
that God is, just, a myth.

The world, for us, intelligent lot,
came to being from a very Big Bang,
the effect of which we had to admit
makes our universe expand.

At first, we thought the Bang was change;
expand, contract, in stable ways.
But now we think of Multiverse,
of which our own a fortunate one,
so fortunate, in fact, it came by chance,
that all things, creatures, found in it,
evolved from some primeval soup.

Some of us are so enraged
and cannot wait to prove these wrong.
We must be better read than this,
to think that bangs, expansions, soups,
and all the chance that give them life,
rise and shine from out of the blue.

Some of us are Creationists,
a name detractors give to us,
who say delusion is our lot;
false religion, false beliefs ,
would not let us face the truth.
If only we would deal with facts
and see the Bible words as myth
perhaps, the truth will dawn on us.

They criticize us just because
we claim our world and we in it,
were made, in truth, in six days flat.
We're told the Bible makes it clear,
as it does so very many other things,
a thousand years of all our days,
are just a day in His account;
and since our day is not His day
it's time we thought again of six.

All and sundry who believe,
including those who don't believe,
surely, all must see it's true -
our own computer, not programmed,
cannot tell its owners name
or things or steps not programmed for.

If God exists, let's speculate;
He or She or It or Else
must be great and quite profound;
or else, we wonder, have to ask,
why Lucifer, so endowed,
as we heard and read in books,
found he knew so little of Him?

Most believers will admit
that naught is known of Him, in truth,
except the things that He reveals -
our lives, our deaths and prophets too,
so many wonders, mysteries -
things we know or yet to know.

Most believers will admit
that the much He has revealed,
at this stage we find ourselves -
we are copies of Himself,
destined to be with Him in time -
baffle, still, our simple minds.

Who can know, it may be true,
that we'll never understand,
no matter what our haste might be,
until our minds have reached His stage,

when we all can be like Him,
and move the mountains as we like?

If you insist and seek to know
where this stage is, the routes to it,
think of Buddha, bless his soul,
who thought your quest a pointless task,
unless it is for life on earth.

Think of Brahman, many more,
incarnations, mindless bliss -
clever thoughts and quite profound -
that, somehow, do not satisfy?

I have my answer which I'm sure
you won't accept or give a care.
It's too simple, too obvious
and that is just the point.
It's the Bible and its words,
which I'm sure will make you laugh.

.There's no lack of expertise,
in Bible talk and all its kinds.
So much preached, so much mixed
in revelation, speculation.
It gets too much, with too many sides,
we all become confused.

Take the deeds of those who preach,
and the examples of their lives.
So unlike His life are theirs,
they cast great doubts on everything,
that those in search of some excuse

are quick to jump on these and say -
there can't be God while this goes on.

What is more, these make us think
that good and bad are, merely, words,
used for things we like, dislike,
and not from any law by God
who, from what we see are done,
has to be a myth.

DEVIL'S TIMES

It is true the Bible said
Satan, soon, will have his time,
when the earth he holds in sway –
a thousand years of Bible time.

After that, the Bible held
Satan, too, will be destroyed,
with his friends and associates,
in a fire worse than Hell.

If it's true I must confess
what I fear for these our times.
With all my flaws, it is my guess
we are smack in Devil's times.

To know these times we kept alive
horror tales of Devil's times,
666 and anti-Christs,
with the Beast and all his mark.

If the demons fun can have

in their state of Hell's torments,
they must have had their time of lives
in our fairy, horror tales.

For while we made our tales of it,
they were busy digging in.
Now these tales are dating fast,
they are among us well entrenched.

But my finger, can it point
or make a guess of things unknown?
Can I ask those who believe
or turn to those who doubt the Book?

GOING ROUND AND ROUND

They have banned religion here,
making God a pointless myth.
All the morals we were taught
are out of date for modern times.

Human Rights is everywhere,
with all freedoms part of it.
It is clear we all have brains;
why, on earth, do we need God?

There are new grounds we can break,
ridding laws of Faith and God.
If these are, somehow, not enough,
we must accept that this is life.

Going round and round and round
in the search for social worth.

Quite confused, all thinking lost,
hither and thither, from pillar to post.

Having naught to guide our lives,
except our modern sense of pride,
we flail around to explain our gripes,
hoping, too, to spice our lives.

Sodomites and single mums,
divorcees and partner chums,
with abortions on demand,
even officers of the law.

We have, just, discovered it;
to be correct in what we say,
no harsh words, whether true or false,
naming evil will incite.

At home, in school and everywhere,
we cannot spank and no cross words;
an ASBO here, an ASBO there,
that will keep the kids behaved.

It is a wise man who said so;
our daily deeds and what they yield
keep our world still spinning round,
to ensure it's not still or we'll die

This the history of the world;
wisdom comes and wisdom goes,
foolishness and follies too
come and go like wisdom does.

FOOLISH THINGS

Does anybody care, these days,
is anybody bothered,
that foolish thinking seems to be everywhere?
All you have to do is, simply, look;
and you may, perhaps, understand why I ask.

Come to think of it, what is foolish;
who is a fool;
who is not or dares to know
if he or she is a fool or not?
Is intelligence not everyone's lot?

If the things we grew up with,
if our ideas of right and wrong are attacked,
laughed at,
and said to be out of date,
are we stung enough to care?

Or if lied to, cajoled and stampeded,
by social and peer pressure,
to acquiesce or even laud deceit,
do we even notice?

Foolish thoughts and actions
lead to pain.
Do we blame it all on Satan,
or like the Unbelievers,
seek refuge in comfort zones,
where belief that such is life,
to be lived and let prevail,
and so acquiesce in many sins?

As our problems sprout,
grow and multiply,
so do camps, factions
and schools of thought,
each with facts,
which support their points of view,
firmly, held.

The oldest row
(it seems every age must have one)
concerns God.
Is He here or there or anywhere?
What can He do, or doesn't or can't do?
And every group and person has a point of view.

According to some, it is Satan spoiling everything,
planting evil thoughts and disbelief
in our minds.
Others think it's us that are Satans,
and some believe it's all myth.

There are those who will ask,
and these are not few,
what, on earth, are foolish things;
who is so wise to take on the burden
of telling anybody
who and what is, or are, foolish?

Indeed, there is, in truth, no answer to them,
or to skeptics pre-convinced,
except, perhaps, for some but not all,
the answers that life provides
through pain and sorrow that are felt.

31

Perhaps, we should pause
and took a long hard look
at our lives,
at our loves, our hates, our appetites,
at the earth
and the world we live in.

Perhaps, we should look, a bit more,
at governments we have
and at all that they do on our behalf.
Maybe, who knows, we may find,
in our lives and deeds,
what is foolish and what is not.

Perhaps, we may, even, learn,
in what our countries and governments do,
which part is foolish and which part not?
Who knows, we may even begin
to understand this earth, this world
and what they mean.

Science is, mercifully, one
of many philosophies,
which, like the others,
has its point of view,
especially,
about knowledge and facts.

It is the most preferred, today,
in our time and age,
because it's based on tested facts,
and has opened our eyes
to many things.

Science is right and will succeed
as long as it, and only if,
is true and pure, and not corrupt;
not misused for selfish ends
or forced on us, by those who will,
cloak in science, its mystique,
their sick, unwholesome, horrible, ways,

Science is false and fraudulent
if its facts are cherry picked,
and used to merge unlikely things,
in evidence that looks like one
but not subjected to its tests.

Science is false and fraudulent
if its truth is based on noise,
and loud propaganda by the Press,
drowning out all genuine facts,
in mass stampede of baseless facts.

You may ask, as you may like,
what is folly, foolishness?
For me it's clear, and clear as clear,
that any science, cherry picked,
is foolishness personified.

Chapter Three

HAVING FUN

Having fun, a popular choice;
having fun has won the day.
There was a time when having fun
was looked askance as something gross,
fit for louts and lay-abouts,
with nothing noble in their sights.

At this time in yesterday,
if you thought of such a thing,
the guilt you felt at such a thought,
your self-respect in danger lane,
made you pause and have a think;
is it right, is it wrong?

I, still, remember how it was
when dads and mums, in great concern,
watched their children seeking fun.
Happiness their main concern,
they made it sure their kids would not
our types of fun to be involved.

See, today, the way it's gone;
our rights and wrongs and all such doubts
are, now, fodders for our pun;
how our taxes, our resource
are spent and wasted in return,
for cleaning up the mess by fun

A few examples will suffice

to tell the tale of having fun.
Getting drunk and smashing cars
is seen, by some, as lots of fun.
Wives and husbands, made cuckolds,
are lots of fun for married folk.

I hear it's now the law;
that male and female, each can be
called a husband or a wife;
that cheating, now, in married state,
is not valid for divorce.

Restless children, ruthless youngsters,
roaming round and round our streets.
Call them YOBs or what you like,
they do, for certain, ruin our lives.
Rudderless kids and teenage mums -
these are products of your fun.

GRAFFITI

Hieroglyphics, Cuneiform,
ancient writings that are gone.
Eggheads, here, are cracking brains
just to know the things they say.

All the knowledge they contain
are hard, intriguing, nuts to crack.
Yet the little we have gained
have made some sense of this our past.

There is still a bit undone
in many lands, in many pasts.

I would have thought these quite enough
to keep our eggheads occupied.

There is a writing of today,
called graffiti by the throng,
widespread here and everywhere,
let us pause and give it thought.

You will see it on the bus,
on its windows and its stops,
on walls and signs and trains and boards,
as long as each can take the chalk.

You may think it's only kids
who create the art because they're bored.
maybe blighters, maybe YOBs,
they are varied as you think.

Give it thought and take a look.
No matter how and where you look,
and though the authors are diverse,
the script and writings look alike.

Dare I call it Devil's script,
from these kids, all poorly raised -
single mums and partner kids?
Let's decipher what it says.

AN OLD DISEASE

An old disease is now in vogue;
young and old are, clearly, smote.
Everywhere, the craze is live,

in the talk, the walk, the life.

The talk is sex, its health and all.
Everybody, sane, must have the lust.
Baring bodies, flouting chests,
makes one sexier than the rest.

Enhanced and upped are female breasts,
not for babies but for sex.
Male and female trousers worn
to an inch of private parts.

Newspapers, too, are full of it:
men and women seeking each.
Gays and lesbians fill the air
with their rights and their campaigns.

Governments, too, have joined the fray,
passing laws that up the pace.
Husband, wife and family, too,
are, now, shameful words to use.

Use the condom, goes the claim,
it fights disease, unwanted babes.
Look, for all their claims, our bill,
more abortions and disease.

Laws they pass to guide our lives.
stretch to clean and strive to wipe,
with a fury that is blind,
tested morals from our minds.

It was our freedom, intellect

that made the rules we, now, resist.
To enable all to co-exist,
we placed our lust, by law, in check.

To change the rules, today's stampede,
to enable sex and all its lusts,
take my word and be assured
will kill our world like those before.

DEVIL'S WORK

When the Bible, that we know
in New Testament, went to town,
it talked and showed, in good detail,
how the demons were expelled.

Believe or not, as you may want,
you can see from what He did,
that many demons, not challenged,
cause the problems of the age.

In every age and every year,
demons come and go with wiles;
causing trouble in our lives,
they make our thinking go berserk.

Their starting point - to dull our minds-
forgetfulness that seizes all.
Sodom, Moloch and its meals
somehow, do not stop our sleep.

Great King Solomon said it all,
under the sun, there's nothing new.

What is now has been before,
our mind was wiped to make it new.

See abortion, now, in vogue
to a Moloch that is vague.
Same sex partners, gay parades
recall the Sodom of the past.

GAYS AND LESBIANS

Gays and lesbians in these times
shut their minds and close their eyes;
private parts that do not fit
do not tell them they are ill.

See our kindness to their plight,
as for those we know are blind,
who do not go about in hype
making joys for being blind.

But the gays will not be told;
lesbians, neither, in their fold.
Egged and pushed by demons now,
they turn our morals upside down.

They will not, their own, conceive;
but win a right to so adopt
a child, by others, well-conceived,
in a logic that is rot.

They have gone as far as can,
putting governments in a can,
making laws and, now, quite mad,

they call it marriage for the lads.

And not content with ruining here,
they seek to spread to other lands
their brand of freedom, human rights
in blackmail deals to countries, poor.

I am surprised, I must admit,
by the Christians, Muslims, Sikhs,
with their Faiths so clear on this,
they stand and stare and nothing kick.

They preach their Faith and fight for turf,
while their lives have nothing much
to do or offer to their Faith,
except contempt for every Faith.

Holiness and sacredness
are the words they use, abuse.
See their lives and what they do;
are they holy in their sins?

Are they gays and lesbians too,
in their closets and pretence?
Why is it they will not speak
while the throng is being deceived?

ABORTION, GAY AND OTHER RIGHTS

Here they are, all senses gone,
so ecstatic in their joy.
Graceful ladies of the past
will now be husbands of their kind.

There is freedom in the air;
and everywhere is choice.
What is wrong or what is right
is, now, determined by our choice.

Most abortions of the past,
were done, in guilt, to save the face,
done in secret but were known
to be wrong and wrong and wrong.

Giving Blacks their civil rights
filled the Whites with empty sighs.
To eat their words was humble pie,
no more Blacks to terrorize.

If we cannot discriminate,
and foist our sickness on the Blacks,
why not, now, we take the chance
and rid ourselves of other hates?

Let us call it Human Rights
and search and find it everywhere;
feminine rights, animal rights,
gay and lesbian, every right.

We can even run to God
to find our rights in what He's done.
What of sex and human life?
There must be rights we can explore.

Tell me, please, what farmer true,
rearing cows or sheep or goats,
will mate the male with male alone,

and be in business in our time.

In this Freedom, it's good sense
and makes you modern, up to date.
Those in shock and their dissent
are homophobes to prosecute.

It's bad enough but there is more,
human reason to the dogs -
babes in wombs are not alive
until we count our twenty weeks!

PAEDOPHILES WILL PAEDOPHOBE

Paedophiles are great concerns;
what a fuss we make of them.
Rocket science it's, certainly, not.
So the fuss we make is aught.

You and I cannot forget,
thirty years ago to date,
when we hyped and when we fussed,
gays and lesbians were the butt.

Homosexuals they were called -
beastly, vile, disgusting types.
Custom, Bible, every thought,
reviled their strange and evil love.

Come today and look around.
Gays and lesbians have their rights.
And those that fussed and their disgust
are homophobes to face the Law.

That is why I prophesy -
give it time and human rights -
homosexuals homophobed
paedophiles will paedophobe.

Chapter Four

EMPIRE DAYS

"Vanity of vanities!"
so said the Preacher,
"all is vanity!"
even if I, too, say it again.

It wasn't that long ago
when European Empires had their go.
Blue eyes, blonde hair, thin lips and a knife edged
nose
made you White even though your skin was ruddy
red.

If you're White, you were made by God;
this was, after all, said so by God;
and all others, like Paradise to Adam,
were made to be at the beck and call of Whites.

The Japanese, the Chinese, they had slanted eyes;
other Asians were either dark or small in size.
Some Indians were red, Levants had hooked their
noses;
Africans, of course, were black, thick lipped and
their noses flat.

Their Science, why, it did its bit
to help explain the things believed.
It found Caucasians, Negroes, Mongoloids
and IQ tests to take along.

It went as far as splitting hairs;
flattened ones, rounded ones and oval ones;
and, although their hair was more like mops,
Golliwogs were better fun.

Looking in back in time, sometimes,
may not keep the world in peace.
Don't mind the Whites and what they say;
they do not want the world in peace.

That may be the reason why
Nels Mandela, Luther King,
and a few that's left unsung,
keep reminding us of God.

Why lament? Why recall?
Have the Whites not seen the light?
Are they not now at their best,
righting wrongs of ages past?

Hares, you know, are free to run;
but to chase is left to hounds.
To run as hares and chase as hounds;
this, my friend, is more than pun.

Now, they've found Democracy,
which the Greeks and, then, their kind,
always thinking we're deceived,
used to, foreign lands, enslave.

Why, on earth, do Africans,
now they see with opened eyes,
throw away their Paradise,

to ape, the Whites, their turbulent earth?

They, now, desert their lands in droves,
exchanging wealth for dubious lives;
oppressed perhaps, in thoughtless haste,
they waste their lives in wintery caves.

These, it seems, are not enough;
well brainwashed, you have no choice.
Black men, now, will plait their hair
to make a point in a pointless cause.

Nat King Cole, he had no choice,
Fitzgerald, Simone or Horne;
with James Brown and Afro hair,
what is wrong with female Blacks?

In slavery times, their kinds were strength;
they kept the faith and race alive.
They were raped and much abused,
but lost no hope or faith in life.

In these times, they've gone berserk;
their equal rights in lion's share.
They make some monkeys of their men
and lose no chance to kill their soul.

How they think, I must admit,
baffles even friendly eyes
Wigs of White hair are preferred
to their obedient, natural hair.

Empire days, maybe, they're gone;

47

think of Greece, think of Rome.
But the mindsets that they leave
seem to live in endless time.

MODERN TIMES

Modern times, that's where we are;
Albert Einstein, and his kind,
keep us baffled with their thoughts-
E is, certainly, mc squared.

Leptons, muons, bosons, gluons,
Higgs, a boson, of his own.
Up down quarks and bottom top quarks,
some are strange, some even charmed.

Energy is dark and matter dark;
and both, we're told, are well conserved.
Gravity waves, they baffle maths.
Our sun is just a ball of gas.

There is Darwin and his kind,
patient, careful, rigorous,
who do their best to make some sense
of our life and being on earth.

Alas, we are but human beings,
in or out of modern times.
There are, always, some of us,
who use his views in blasphemy.

We can't forget the medical men
who, for sure, do save more lives

than those of us who will be God,
who clone and stem cell, trifling life.

Where on earth will all these be,
if ignored, the digital kids?
What appliance, what we do,
is not based on what they do?

What of governments of the world,
who cheat and lie to stay on top,
who make democracy a kind of god,
yet don't believe in it one jot.

There's the Press, both, free or fair,
in papers, TV and the air.
They make a lot about free Press,
but cause the problems of the times.

All the achievements of our times,
in spite of all that we have got,
it seems that we are in a pot,
overheating, about to burst.

Our past achievements, we can see,
were built on blood and wickedness.
Our pot has burst in recent times,
in the first and second Wars.

It looks like time is ripe again
for the boiling pot to burst.
Wars and bombings everywhere,
safety valves not quite enough.

Things are hard in modern times.
No surprise that this is so.
Faith in God has lost its shine.
There is no anchor to our lives.

SOCIALISM AND THE REST

I can see the reason now
why there's angst in every place.
Some are rich and some are poor;
but that's not why there's so much angst.

They say they're civilised.
They say they're fair to all.
But look around at all they do
and see the people in the moon.

The Greeks were civilised;
it turns out Helots were not so.
Romans, too, were civilised;
countless slaves, they thought not so.

Egypt, Persia, kingdoms then;
all of them were civilised.
The only people just nowhere
were my people, Africans.

My! It's great to civilise,
living cheek by jowl all day.
You learn your manners, tolerance,
and how delightful are the arts.

You can kill and go to war

and rob and pillage in the act.
As long as you have won the war
you are very civilised.

Take it down to modern times
to Europe, US and their kinds.
There, they call it civil rights,
voting rights and human rights.

If these are true, it must be right
to live in joy without a fear.
Those in this deceit believe
are just living in the clouds.

Truth is fact and fact is clear;
we are living in their cells.
These cells are prisons without walls;
but more secure than those with walls.

They make a lot of noise of these;
freedom, rights, in all their shades.
But what we really have and face
is a wicked Total State.

There's no right, there's no wrong.
There's no slack in deed or thought.
What is right or what is wrong
is the economy and it's jobs.

So the poor in their despair
clutch at straws to save themselves.
The straw they catch is straight and weak;
hate and envy for the rich.

So they spend their lives in vain
seeking wealth or fighting it.
Socialism and all the rest
claim to be tools for the useless fight.

Oh my poor, my, Africa,
you knew it all before their time.
To live with nature and its mores
is the wisest act of time.

There is blemish in everything;
there's a wart on every face.
The logs before their eyes in spite;
they made a lot about your specks.

Fret not now about your state.
Do not moan about the past.
You must beware, their wickedness,
and disregard their arrogance.

There's a truth you must accept;
there's no hope for a peaceful man
among a people, drunk with wars,
egged and urged by desperate wants.

DEMOCRACY

Democracy, what, on earth, is it?
Democracy, who, on earth, believes in it?
They say some people do.

If it is what they say;
that democracy is the best form of government;

which provides a level playing field,
and protects the weak from the strong

Then, governments, ancient and modern,
north, south, east and west, everywhere,
none, I've found, believes in it.

Priviledged, ancient, thoughtful, Greeks,
who denied Helots their rights and votes,
get the credit for inventing it.

Europeans, governments and their elite,
who didn't think women or the landless
fit to vote,
are champions of democracy.

European dissidents or convicts,
forced, desperate or willing immigrants to the
Americas,
who killed off the local inhabitants,
are champions of democracy.

Recent Americans, north or south,
who didn't think the natives,
or their African slaves,
fit to vote,
are champions of democracy.

Poor democracy, championed by all;
poor democracy, unchanged,
apparently, unchangeable in any age,
used by those in power,
to do whatever they want to do.

There used to be elections;
there used to be votes;
in a democracy.
At least, that is what we were told.

The majority used to have its way,
the minority its say,
in a democracy.
At least, that is what we were told.

But now it's the noisiest, not the right,
nor the majority,
who have both their way and say.

In this great Democracy,
fringe, minority, dangerous groups,
worm their way and seize control
of the TV, Press and all.
They win elections, pass their laws,
using PR, mass deceits.

If there is democracy, the kind they push,
for us to believe,
why can't the Irish vote, instead of fight,
to be one or two?

If there is democracy, the kind they push,
for us to believe,
why can't the Kurds vote, instead of fight,
to be in or out of Iran, Iraq or Turkey?

If there is democracy, the kind they push,
for us to believe,

why is there fighting, and not votes,
in Iraq, in Afghanistan and now Syria,
not to talk of Libya?

If there is democracy, the kind they push,
for us to believe,
why can't gays, lesbians and straights vote
to have their separate ways in law;
than have the taxes paid by each
fund the other's ways and different lives?

If there is democracy, the kind they push,
for us to believe,
why can't the racists, bigots, nudists, and all vote
to live their lives as they would choose,
as long as each will not be kept,
by the wealth and labour
of those despised or who despise.

If there is democracy, the kind they push,
for us to believe,
why are taxes and tax rates different
for different and democratic,
citizens of the place
without the vote of the mainstream throng?

If there is democracy, the kind they push,
for us to believe,
why don't we get the majority to agree,
disagree
on one, or different, personal allowance,
for all income tax,
on one, or different, corporate allowance,

for all company tax?

If there is democracy, the kind they push,
for us to believe,
why don't we get the majority to agree,
disagree
on one or different tax rate,
the same or different exceptions, incentives,
for personal income, and company, tax?

If there is democracy, the kind they push,
for us to believe,
why can't many more, than I can name,
vote
to be whatever they want to be
or want to have   ?

No, it is not democracy yet;
at least, not the one they push.

LEADING MEN

Those who lead and those they lead,
be they presidents or just me,
vie, in everywhere I know,
to have their names in great renown.

They are there in Africa,
in north and south America,
Europe, Asia near and far,
and the places that are far.

Take a look at how they lead;

pause to look at those they lead,
you will not need me to tell
who is leading, following well.

All of us have got one life;
we cannot waste or play with it.
If you lead or you are led,
each of us must get the best.

A leader is bad and terrible job,
who shirks the duty of his job.
To give the welfare due to all
is a duty owed to all.

BLACK AFRICANS

There are people that I know,
who, in numbers, make one fifth.
Most of them, as you may know,
live their lives in Africa;
while a few of them, I guess,
live in every place on earth.

They are such that you can say
very good slaves they, often, make.
Hanged and raped or mauled in jest,
forced or willing, they will serve.

To raise a fist in self defence,
is not, somehow, in their psyche.
But, if, by chance, they're free to rule,
their prime delight to oppress their kind.

So, it is in every age,
ancient, middle, modern age,
empires, kingdoms, take your pick,
slaves they are to buy and sell.

UNITED NATIONS

U. N. here, U. N. there;
U.N.O. is everywhere.
Is it health? Is it peace?
U. N. O. is there to please.

Sixty years it is today,
when, in wake of World War II,
those victorious formed a group
to seek a better route to peace.

At first it seemed that this would work
when the victors made the rules.
But if it had to keep the rules,
it had to give a voice to all.

Taking countries that are fakes,
it made its first and great mistake.
No exclusions were allowed;
even those its rules maligned.

Human rights it had as base.
democracy was its quest.
But many of them in U. N. O.
have no respect for each of these.

Those that other Faiths deny

to their country and their folk,
there they are in U. N. O.,
making noise and casting votes.

Wicked soldiers, with the gun,
who take the land and all by force;
see them pose as heads of state,
while the U. N. looks away.

If the U. N. is for peace,
if its purpose is for real,
it must make, and keep it too,
its own rules and charters true.

WHEN YOU SAY THE UNO

When you say the UNO,
what you mean is USA.
When you hear the world has said,
what you mean is the West has said.

Jesus Christ was good and just;
He came to set the world aright.
What He left behind to grow
was highly jacked by the desperate West.

It helped the West to rob and kill,
in a conscience clear as mud.
Crushing cultures, scorching fields,
scorching all in heartless greed.

The West provokes, attacks and kills,
all behind its Christian shield.

Let the victims dare complain;
the West lambasts them, devilish foes.

Poor Sadam was made by them,
Laden, Nasser, many more.
When these fools, alas, awake,
they are hounded, killed, as dogs.

See the South and North Korea,
slaves and pawns in Western games.
Head or tails, up comes the West
who sells the tools of war and peace.

As the US tests its planes,
and tanks and troops and maneuvers,
North Korea must stand and watch
or else is drunk and mongering war.

Nuclear plants and bombs and planes;
children's toys in Western lands.
No one else can have these toys;
or the world will have to end.

Facts confuse the Western Press,
whose mind is made up from the start.
They will besmirch and smear and tar
victims who defend themselves.

MAKING POVERTY HISTORY

Great Bob Geldof, great pop stars;
human beings with hearts of gold,
though with lives of gain and gold,

they give a thought to those that starve.

They have, time and time again,
to soften hearts that's made of stone,
used their tools and ways of life
to make the people, leaders, care.

There're the governments of the West,
(and those of East that do not care),
who, in bid to get the votes,
chase as hounds and run like hares.

There's the governments of the lands,
who will let their people starve.
Gangsters more than leaders there,
they have no shame, remorse or heart.

In spite of all the aid they get
from Bob Geldof and his set,
their game, it seems, is get some more
by pushing things from bad to worse.

So they make a point of it,
to make their countries decrepit.
They use their twisted minds and zest
to dupe their allies from the West.

If we, really, truly, aim
"making poverty history" true,
then we must, I think, agree
that governments there must be to serve.

But, how do we, in this our time,

go to countries, sovereign,
and force a government of our kind
on countries which are sovereign?

Hear me out, I must insist
that all we need is what exists-
U. N. rules and their effects
in these countries that we help.

I cannot hide it anymore;
all these countries we must save
are just tribes by West corralled
and named as countries of their make.

Such fake countries cannot work,
because their scoundrels will exploit
their tribal base to get on top
and pose, for sure, as heads of state.

If we do not do things right,
and call referendum in the tribes,
to choose the country of their choice,
poverty, history, not a hope.

I MUST MIGRATE OR ELSE I'LL DIE

Wuthering Heights of English lore,
scraggy peaks and snowy caps,
mountain faces, sheer and low,
from Ben Nevis to the Alps,
have chased away our rounded hills.

Our green verdure and hot terrains,

with storms and thunders and their rains;
our floods and torrents, with their slopes,
our snakes and tigers, antelopes,
have run before their tender sheep.

Their healthy cows, with so much milk,
with cheese and joints and rounded chucks,
have made our rhinos and our crocs,
our goats and chimps and all their ilk,
things vexatious, tedious jobs.

I hear you talk about my deeds,
without one thought about my needs.
Where were you, my friend indeed,
when in love with rounded hills,
I went to enjoy the green verdure?

I sought the sun to warm my bones.
I thought the fruits were good and due.
I saw the brook to cool my domes.
But I was bitten by the snake;
and chased by tigers on the take.

The rhinos thought me very much game.
All the insects bit the same.
The crocs would not, even, let me know.
It's just by luck that I was saved
by their seasons and their snow.

I looked around and found out too
their snakes are pets and do not bite.
Their tigers, lions, live in zoos.
Why, my friend, the ballyhoo?

I must migrate or else I'll die

VIOLENT TRIBES

Violent tribes have met their match
in talk, in boasts, in evil deeds.
Quite unlike the timid blacks
slaughtered, bullied, left to bleed.

Though in Christ they all professed,
building churches, monuments,
their code of life was split in sets,
White and Black and each his set.

Quoting Christ in all their deeds,
with their lives their proof of it,
they built a fortune of their kind
from the land and blood of Blacks.

There are those who give their life
in great Jihads for Paradise.
Their code of life and way of truth
are from Allah, no dispute.

What is it they call these things?
Karma? Vengeance of the gods?
It will torture and may kill
those its dos and don'ts ignore.

See these tribes that were the parts
of the business in the Blacks;
their views of God in commerce lost
in crudes and oils to be got.

See them now at each their throats,
evils, ghastly, now unfold.
Suicides, bombs and deaths *en masse*;
violent tribes have met their kind.

THE WEST HAS LOST ITS MIND

The West has lost its mind;
the West has lost its sense;
the West has lost its everything;
the West is ripe for war.

The ideas that saved the West;
the ideas that built the West;
the ideas that gave the West its might;
the West delights to dump.

There was truth and telling it,
which the West explained to all.
We all believed; we saw it work;
now the West has lost it all.

Fair was fair and right was right;
that was why the West was might.
Now the West has lost the plot;
fair and right are compromised.

Men will sleep with other men;
so will women, too, the same.
They kill their babies in their wombs
and call it Choice and Human Rights.

The old complain of pain and life,

and seek to end it all by choice.
Afraid of life and certain death,
they kill their young to stem cell life.

Nobody knows from whence we came,
or where we go when all these end.
This has made us speculate
a thousand hows and whys and whens.

But the Jews, they had their tale,
just like other tribes we know,
each as sure as sure can be,
of where we came from, where we go.

So intrigued was all the West
with the Christian side of it,
they rushed and took it as their own,
and robbed and killed because of it.

Now satiated, full of it,
the West is fed up and aghast.
Obsessed with pleasure, newly thoughts,
they rush to wipe out Christian thoughts.

Chapter Five

SHAM, SHAM, SHAM

Marriage then, marriage now,
Marriage, Oh, is just a sham.
What a shame it is a sham;
marriage, yes, is just a sham.

When the ancients ran to it,
did they, really, have a choice?
What, on earth, can deal with lust,
a raging fire, easily lit?

Sodom, Lesbos, sought its end;
but they failed, it didn't work.
Spartans, Soviets sought its end;
too, they failed, it didn't work.

All the Faiths have done their bit,
preaching love and training minds,
with some sanctions here and there;
yet it doesn't work.

In this age of Human Rights,
with rights and freedoms free to all,
to male and female and their rights;
still, it doesn't work.

Ancient, modern, future times;
there is nothing that's untried.
What, on earth, is left undone

with love and marriage and their lusts?

EMPTY SPOUSES

I know a husband and his wife.
I know a husband with no wife.
I know a wife who lost her man.
I know them all and all their plans.

I heard it said, the spouse is dear;
your friend, your love, your confidant.
Your fears, your hopes, your secret thoughts
are known and shared by you alone.

But, now, I hear the genuine spouse
is blank and shallow, stone wall like.
And all their friends are their secrets,
with all the things they do or share.

"I have my fears, my secret fears.
I have my tastes, those childish joys.
Sometimes, too, I fall in love;
you do not think I'll tell my spouse.

A lovely spouse is there for peace;
what peace is there if my spouse should know?
I know this peace is Devil's peace.
But that's the one the world would own."

That, now, the spouse will swear in fiat:
"I do not cheat my spouse in faith.
To give my love and all my laugh -
why, my friend! I'll be a mat!"

With all of this, they fret and strive
to find a way to bear their life,
not knowing, really, what they are -
empty spouses here and there.

I'VE HAD ENOUGH OF LOVE

I've had enough of love.
I've had enough from this your love.
I've had enough of claims for it.
I've had it here with it.

There's a lot that's made of love
which, in fact, is bonk.
All the things they say it's got
is nothing but a load of tosh.

There's a saying that we know-
all is fair in love and war.
This, itself, should make us know
of the love we should beware.

If it's love we know is God's,
then I will rejoice.
In His love, the moon and sun
are as constant and for all.

All our weather, seasons, times
are, all, faithful to their time.
The rains that fall and sun that shines
are the same for good and bad.

But take the love that we enthuse;

and take a look at what is gained.
In marriage, friendship, neighbourhood,
it is the cause of pain.

See two people fall in love,
their life aglow with lots of shine.
Come back there in six months' time
and you will find two broken pots.

Take the love that there exists
between those their marriage done.
Come and see the way they cheat;
it makes you wonder what they love.

These cheats, themselves, are not that safe
from more cheating by their mates.
Branding what they do as love,
they call their tortures all of love.

Why not pause and now admit
that what we name, and hold as love,
is not love but lust for sex,
which is never satisfied.

THE RIGHT APPROACH

Hurrah! I've got the right approach!
I'll talk. I'll do. I'll drink my fill.
I'll take and cheat and lie and kill,
for these are things that go with it,
when you have the right approach.

The years I worked! In vain I toiled

to help my friends and foes alike.
I sought the good of all I met,
but all it did was bring regret.
You see? I lacked the right approach.

When you have the right approach,
you'll know the time to play the hurt.
You'll know the time to be a sport,
to give no gifts or do a turn;
and, still, they'll think you're lots of fun.

You'll learn to tap the ego talk
and use the ear to free the tongue.
In all your talk, no right or wrong;
no thief, condemned, will bear your talk.
And this is true in right approach.

You get to learn and act it too
that people living, bad and good,
do not care to think or check
the things you say or do or fake,
so long as you will ride their horse.

The good and bad, alike, you'll find
will die for you or sell their kind,
for things they hate and swore to quell.
And when for you, they'd rush to hell,
you'll know you've got the right approach.

MR. GOODMAN

I am a good man, very good man;
and that is why I die.

What is due I give to all,
though, nobody, ever, gives me mine.

I labour so much not to hurt;
but every time, they want me hurt.
I do resent when gossip flies;
I hear you too when, thus, maligned.

But me, I'm smeared without an end
and tarred without a thought or word.
Naught I do is, ever, strange;
naught beyond my wont to do.

I do abhor the telling of lies;
but me, I'm lied to all the time.
To cheat I fly and rather die;
but me, to cheat they rush and vie.

I'd rather faint, that extra mile,
to avoid deceit of friend or foe.
But everyone I meet to know
deceives me, just a matter of time.

The whole of me I make to give
in friendliness and all I have.
But see the gift I, always, get
to show that they resent my best.

All I have I give in love,
but I receive in bowls of hate.
Only my friends, in this our life,
have problems, not me. How can I?

My friends, alone, are ill, not I.
My friends, alone, are, ever, broke.
My friends, alone, have work to do.
And all I have is idle time.

When I'm dead, I'm sure to hear
how my friends will ask in pain;
why I could not come to share
all the things they bear in vain.

What kind of friend, they'd ask, am I
who cannot come to aid his friends?
And this is just to come and mix
and, then, be lost amidst their crowd.

I did not wake and rise, though dead,
to give their honour to my friends.
See? Don't you? It's all my fault;
I'm not a good man, not at all.

FOR A WALK

The wind has, truly, got my heart.
In wonder, new, I'm born.
This must be the moon I've known,
the air, the skies, the earth.

So soft and tender in these lights,
so cool and fresh the airs.
Your eves, Nsukka, in July,
your eves a joy to fly.

Alone, I, really, thought I was.

So full of worries, I was sure.
Now, I know how blind I was
to your presence and your love.

Oh my gosh! My sights are new.
With fairy joys I gloat.
Who knows when all these will be loathe,
or when I look and cannot see?

The call to me is from afar.
The air is better over there.
My tired legs have found the strength
to let me roam and let me spend.

The head is light, I feel it well.
My limbs are lithe, it's not just talk.
The urge, perhaps, of tramps, I guess.
I say I want a walk.

I THANK YOU, GOD

I thank you, God, for creating me
and placing me, here, where I am.
I thank you, God, for letting me
see and live and taste this life.

I thank you, God, that I was there
when the past, the present, changed.
I thank you, God, that I am here
as the future now unfolds.

I thank you, God, that I recall
those I lived with, met and heard;

tears and joys and memories,
at the edges of the past.

I thank you, God, that I have seen
decent, honest, happy folk,
who would have done a better job
of what we have, misuse, today.

I thank you, God, that I did see
those, whose faith the skies would reach,
who, in spite of all their spunk,
were just smothered by the times.

I thank you, God, for those I knew,
Tony, Simon, Lolonta.
I thank you, God, for what I heard,
Nnoro, Mgbeke, Obidegwu.

Index of First Lines

www.ingramcontent.com/pod-product-compliance
Lightning Source LLC
Chambersburg PA
CBHW070544030426
42337CB00016B/2349